ANSWERING

GOD'S
CALL

Other Books by Barbara Lee

God Isn't Finished with Me Yet:
Discovering the Spiritual Graces of Later Life

ANSWERING

GOD'S CALL

a
SCRIPTURE-BASED
JOURNEY
for
Older Adults

BARBARA LEE

LOYOLA PRESS.
A JESUIT MINISTRY
Chicago

LOYOLA PRESS.
A JESUIT MINISTRY

3441 N. Ashland Avenue
Chicago, Illinois 60657
(800) 621-1008
www.loyolapress.com

© 2021 Barbara Lee
All rights reserved.

Scripture texts in this work are taken from the *New American Bible*, revised edition
© 2010, 1991, 1986, 1970 Confraternity of Christian Doctrine,
Washington, D.C., and are used by permission of the copyright owner. All rights
reserved. No part of the *New American Bible* may be reproduced in any form
without permission in writing from the copyright owner.

Cover art credit: Loyola Press, billnoll/E+/Getty Images, Pinghung Chen/EyeEm/
Getty Images, KjellBrynildsen/E+/Getty Images
Back cover author photo, Rebecca MB Pearson.

ISBN: 978-0-8294-5131-3
Library of Congress Control Number: 2020949658

Printed in the United States of America.
21 22 23 24 25 26 27 28 29 30 Versa 10 9 8 7 6 5 4 3 2 1

Clearly, we elders at this time and moment of our lives need to reinvent ourselves, because old age, as it is today, is a new phenomenon.

—Pope Francis

Contents

Introduction

In the early 1980s, the law firm of which I was a partner was going through a major restructuring, and the future was uncertain for all of us. I needed to make an informed decision about my own course of action, without much clarity about what my options were, let alone how they might accord with my spiritual life. My spiritual director at the time suggested that I make the Spiritual Exercises of St. Ignatius in the form of the Retreat in Daily Life, also known as the Nineteenth Annotation. That was my introduction to Ignatian spirituality and in particular to praying with Scripture.

Somehow, I found time, while still meeting litigation deadlines, to see my director regularly on Tuesday evenings between Advent and Pentecost. That improbable scheduling achievement was the first grace I experienced with the Exercises. What I remember most clearly, forty years on, is learning to pray with Scripture. The graces of that experience have stayed with me ever since.

One of the meditations that resonated with me was the story of Moses in Exodus 3:1–7:7. God was calling him to do something extraordinary, and all he could say was *BUT*—the word he used to introduce each of a long litany of objections. Was I doing the same thing? How often do we respond to God's call with "But . . ."?

Another passage that left a lasting impression was the call of Joseph, in Matthew 1:18–24. The angel appeared to Joseph in a dream; there was no conversation. In fact, nowhere in the Gospels is Joseph quoted as saying a single word. Instead, it is silence that lets us hear what God is saying to us. Joseph is a role model of that interior stillness that draws us closer to God.

Many years later, when I began a ministry of spiritual direction to the aging, I realized that these two passages had another important element in common. Moses was eighty years old when he finally accepted God's call. We don't know Joseph's age, but tradition depicts him as an older man. Both of them are role models for older adults as we are called by God to new forms of discipleship. There are many other such role models in both the Hebrew Bible and the New Testament, men and women whose later-life experiences can inspire us in the twenty-first century. Anna, for example, was eighty-four; Abram was seventy-five; Elizabeth was "in her old age." God did not write any of them off as "too old" for witness, for trust, or for rejoicing.

In our society that emphasizes, even fetishizes, youth, there are few spiritual role models for older adults. We often feel invisible. Praying with the biblical stories of men and women who grew closer to God in their later years may help correct that imbalance—as well as introduce the riches of praying with Scripture to those who may not yet have experienced it.

1

The Call to Discipleship

We are all called to discipleship, at every stage of our lives. The call to follow Jesus, to live as he taught us to live, and to grow in holiness does not end when we retire from paid work, when our children leave home, or when other major life changes occur. But for older adults—a term I find more respectful than "the elderly" or "senior citizens"—the call often changes. God calls us to holiness in new ways. We have gifts that are particular to our later years, especially the wisdom that comes from experience. We also have age-related challenges, such as how to cope with retirement, downsizing, and various kinds of losses. We need spiritual resources to use our gifts and meet those challenges. This book explores one such resource: praying with the Scripture stories of men and women who experienced calls to discipleship as older adults.

Who are "older adults"? There is no specific defining age. When I have given retreats at parishes and at assisted-living

1

facilities, I have met fragile people in their fifties as well as vibrant, active people in their eighties and nineties. What they have in common is one or more life-changing experiences, which can occur at almost any age but become increasingly likely the older we get. These are some of the people I am referring to:

Retirees. People in our society are so often defined by work: "What do you do?" is a common icebreaker. For those who no longer "do" something for pay, the question may sting. That pain can be multiplied for anyone whose retirement wasn't voluntary.

Empty nesters. Especially when grown children live at a distance and the demands of their work or their own family obligations prevent them from making frequent visits, parents' feelings may be very similar to those of the newly retired.

Caregivers. Women—and it is usually women—in their sixties and older increasingly find themselves principal caregivers for parents in their eighties and nineties, or for a disabled spouse. There is little preparation for the physical and emotional demands of such a role, and often there is little or no access to support groups or other resources. The parents of disabled children who may outlive them also have added burdens. So too do those who have responsibilities for grandchildren whose parents are working long hours or have medical problems of their own.

Widows and widowers. Those who have lost a spouse face some of the same experiences as the other subgroups, which are often greatly intensified by the pain of loss and uncertainty.

People with the physical limitations that come with age. Diminished vision or hearing, the need for a walker or an oxygen tank, or more serious disabilities can be devastating for people who must give up activities that have been important to them in the past.

The seriously ill and the dying. Residents of nursing homes and patients in hospitals do not always receive compassionate care and often must listen to platitudes from younger people who have no idea what they are going through.

Experiences such as these present more than inevitable losses. And they often trigger an identity crisis: Who am I *now*? Many people also experience a spiritual crisis: Where is the grace in this? Or even more starkly: How do I pray about this?

At retreats and in individual spiritual direction, people have often told me that the ways they are accustomed to praying don't seem to nourish them anymore. Some expressly ask for help in finding new ways to pray as they enter a new stage of their lives. In an attempt to meet that expressed need, this book focuses on one approach that has proved fruitful for people of all ages and stages of life: the Ignatian tradition of praying with Scripture. This way of praying seems to me to be a particularly good resource for anyone facing major life changes. For older adults, it can furnish role models to enrich our prayer and celebrate the blessings of aging.

The Bible offers many examples of men and women who were called to live new forms of discipleship, new ways of holiness, in later life. The stories presented here, from the Hebrew Bible and the New Testament, illuminate different ways that people were called to later-life discipleship and how they responded. In Christian churches, many of their stories are included in the Sunday readings during the liturgical year. Some of these people, such as Anna, Simeon, Elizabeth, and Joseph, are very familiar, yet rarely does a homily or commentary focus on what it means to experience a late call such as the one each of them heard. Others, such as Miriam, Lydia, and the widow of Zarephath, might be less familiar.

My hope is that the newness of their stories may help lead the reader to new insights.

All the Scripture passages I have included, and the prayer suggestions that follow each of them, are the fruits of my own prayer and, in many cases, material I have included in retreat presentations. Each one has been chosen because it helps us reflect, not on what we *do*, but on who we *are*, now, at this stage of life. A deeper understanding of who we are should lead us to appreciate our unique gifts and how God is calling us to live them: in prayer, in service to others, and in looking to the future with hope.

We all have different gifts, but some are shared by many older adults:

The gift of wisdom. Pope Francis, himself an older adult, has often spoken about the role of this age group in the community: the need for greater interaction between old and young, the responsibility of caring for the marginalized, and above all the valuable and often overlooked contributions of older adults to church and society. Addressing a group on December 16, 2017, he said this:

> The elderly are the historical memory of every community, a patrimony of wisdom and faith that needs to be heard, cared for and valued. . . . [T]hey have wisdom,

life's wisdom, history's wisdom, the homeland's wisdom, the family's wisdom. And we need all this!

That's a little different from the message we get from secular society, in which older people are often invisible.

Native Americans, as well as many other non-Eurocentric cultures, have traditionally venerated the oldest among them and placed great value on their wisdom. Our youth-oriented culture in the developed world, with its rapidly changing language, music, fads, fashions, and technology, is diametrically opposed to such a worldview. Yet older people still have greater wisdom than the young, no matter what messages we might receive from television or social media. Our prayer should help us rediscover the gift of wisdom and find new ways to use it.

The gift of interior freedom. As we age, many of us who are no longer free to do some of the things we used to enjoy discover that we have more *interior freedom:* from the responsibilities of job and family, from the pressure to succeed, from all the getting and spending. This in turn can help us discern our individual gifts—the ones we used in doing our jobs or raising our children, for example. What, exactly, are we now free to do, to be?

The gift of prayer. Many older adults find themselves called to a deeper life of prayer, especially if circumstances have given them more time and opportunity. This may lead to a greater awareness of graces we have taken for granted, or simply a closer relationship with a loving God. For some people, this may be a very specific answer to the question "Who am I now?"

The gift of the possible. There is no escaping the diminishment that comes with age. When we can no longer drive, or when we have outlived people we have loved, it is all too easy to focus on what we have lost. This is the time to ask, "Where is the grace in this?" Some people are led to explore various kinds of creativity, in art or music or working with their hands. People who enjoyed gardening or photography or some other activity as a hobby or release from tension may be able to appreciate more fully the creativity that is a gift from God. Others find satisfaction and grace in volunteer service, especially the kind that helps the needy. Still others are called to do things they never would have imagined. God is full of surprises!

We may not be called to such extraordinary things as Anna or Abram were, but in praying with these Scripture passages, we may be given the grace to develop a deeper understanding of our own call.

How to Use This Book

Each of the following chapters has three parts. The first is the text of a Scripture passage illustrating a later-life call. Each passage is quoted in full in order to make it possible to pray without needing to consult a separate Bible. There follows a discussion of the background, which is intended as an aid to prayer, not a scholarly commentary. Each chapter concludes with "prayer starters," suggestions intended to help the reader pray about the passage and discern what God is saying about its application to his or her own life. In some cases, where a psalm seems especially relevant to the subject of the chapter, it is reproduced in full. In other instances, other Scripture passages that might be useful supplements to the theme are referred to but not quoted.

"Suggestions" is the operative word here. No one can tell you what graces you might experience in praying with a particular Scripture. Some passages may not resonate with you at all; others may be instruments of grace that go far beyond anything mentioned in these prompts. This structure is best adapted to reading and praying over one chapter at a time rather than reading the whole book cover-to-cover.

Roman Catholics who received religious education before the Second Vatican Council—that is, people like me who were born before World War II, as well as most baby boomers—had very little exposure to the Bible beyond what was read at Sunday Mass. Laypeople were often discouraged from reading the Bible, lest they adopt subjective interpretations at odds with church teaching. New translations and greater availability of adult religious education after the Second Vatican Council heralded a refreshing new approach to making this great resource more widely available. Yet for many people who came of age too soon to have benefited from this approach, the Bible remained a closed book.

Praying with Scripture opens it up. No formal study or previous experience is needed. There is nothing intimidating about it. For those who are new to this way of praying, a brief introduction is in order.

When we pray with Scripture, we are using not only our minds but also our hearts. Our goal is to take the living Word of God into our hearts and to listen with our hearts to what God is saying to us.

There are two main approaches to this kind of prayer. One focuses on *images* and is sometimes called imaginative prayer or Ignatian contemplation. The other focuses on *words* and is called *lectio divina*, usually translated as "holy reading."

Whole books have been written about each of these forms of prayer; here is a brief introductory summary.

Praying with Images: Imaginative Prayer

1. Place yourself in the presence of God. Ask for the grace to listen with your heart. Read the passage of Scripture a few times, slowly and attentively.

2. Picture the scene described in the passage. Imagine yourself as one of the people in the story, for example, a person healed by Jesus, one of the disciples, or a member of Abram's family.

   - What do you see?
   - Who is present, and what are they doing, where?
   - What do you hear?
   - How do you feel?
   - What do you want to say to God about what you're experiencing?
   - What is God saying to you about it?

3. Talk to God about what you have experienced. End with a prayer of thanksgiving and/or the Lord's Prayer. Record your thoughts and feelings in your spiritual journal.

Praying with the Word: *Lectio Divina*

1. Follow step 1 as in "Praying with Images: Imaginative Prayer," above.

2. Is there a word or phrase that stands out? Sit with the word or phrase; savor it; reflect on how it speaks to you. What does this word or phrase suggest that God is saying to you? What does it move you to say to God?

3. Follow step 3 as in "Praying with Images: Imaginative Prayer," above.

Some people may prefer to pray with words. Others are much more comfortable with visual images. Still others find appeal in both approaches. All will probably find that some Scripture passages are more suitable to one method or the other.

The Gospels include many stories of healing, forgiveness, and miracles, such as Jesus feeding the five thousand or stilling the storm at sea. In Roman Catholic, Anglican, and Lutheran churches that use the Revised Common Lectionary, passages of this kind are read on most of the ordinary Sundays of the year between Pentecost and Advent. They offer a rich cast of characters with whom we might identify and situations in which we can place ourselves without difficulty. On the Sundays immediately after Easter, by contrast, we hear Gospels that draw on Jesus' last message to his disciples on the night before he died. These passages emphasize peace, love, and the coming of the Holy Spirit—words that invite us to probe their depths.

The reflection on Elizabeth in chapter 15 is an example of imaginative prayer. Some of the passages about eternal life referred to in chapter 21 may be well suited to *lectio divina*. In either of these approaches, the important thing to remember is that we are communicating with a God who loves us. Communication is a two-way process. We listen to the living Word of God and bring to God all our thoughts and feelings and concerns.

The quotations in this book are from the *New American Bible*, Revised Edition. In Roman Catholic churches in the United States, the readings at Mass are from this translation. Bibles are available in many print formats, downloadable versions, and e-books. Since e-readers offer a choice of type sizes, modern technology may offer a way around the small type in many print Bibles.

2

Who Do You Say That I Am?

The questions of identity that often accompany aging inevitably affect our spiritual lives, specifically how God is now calling us to live our faith. Most of us approach this question with a more mature understanding of God than we had in our younger years. In praying with Scripture—indeed with any form of prayer—it is always a good idea to start with a review of how we see God and then move on to how God sees us.

Who Is God for You?

Scripture: Luke 9:18–20

> Once when Jesus was praying in solitude, and the disciples were with him, he asked them, "Who do the crowds say that I am?" They said in reply, "John the Baptist; others, Elijah; still others, 'One of the ancient prophets has arisen.'" Then he said to them, "But who do you say that I am?" Peter said in reply, "The Messiah of God."

Jesus' question seems to have taken most of the disciples by surprise. They gave a variety of answers: John the Baptist, Elijah, or "one of the ancient prophets." A prophet was a good guess among educated Jews, who were familiar with the prophetic tradition in Israel's history and were comfortable with the idea of God's word being revealed through prophets. Jesus as the new Elijah was more surprising, because there is no indication that the Jews of Jesus' time believed in reincarnation.

The people the disciples were quoting were not alone in their confusion. In the early chapters of Luke, there are a number of familiar scenes that emphasize recognition of the divinity of Jesus. Mary was told in so many words that the child to be born of her would be the Son of God (Luke 1:35).

The shepherds were told that "a savior has been born for you who is Messiah and Lord" (Luke 2:11). And when Mary and Joseph brought the child to the Temple to fulfill the requirements of Jewish law, he was recognized by not one but two God-centered laypeople, Simeon and Anna (Luke 2:22–38).

The prominence of these recognition scenes suggests that Jesus was first encountered as a very ordinary-appearing human baby. The adult Jesus must also have been seen as an ordinary rabbi—until people personally experienced his authentic teaching and his healing power.

Peter did—and when Jesus asked him, "Who do *you* say that I am?" he answered without hesitation: the Messiah.

That term had tremendous emotional significance for religious Jews of the time. They were expecting the deliverance of Israel from its enemies rather than the spiritual deliverance that is our Christian understanding. For most Christians today, "Messiah" is a more or less abstract term, not one that figures in the way they address God in prayer. Many other titles that are traditionally applied to God are abstract: "Creator," "Redeemer," "Sanctifier," "Yahweh." It isn't always easy to address our prayer to someone with one of these names.

Some of the more concrete terms we use in prayer present different problems. Some people are uncomfortable with "Lord" because of its association with feudal class society.

"Father" can evoke strong emotions, positive or negative. For example, people who have had absent or abusive parents may have trouble calling God "Father." Many others find great comfort in picturing God as a loving parent.

When I ask my spiritual directees how they see God, I hear a variety of answers. Many people say Jesus; some say God the Father. Few people mention the Holy Spirit initially, although awareness of the Spirit often emerges when they speak of their prayer in more detail. One man told me he prayed to Mary more than to God. For me, it is the Jesus of the Gospels I visualize in prayer.

PRAYER STARTERS

1. To whom do you address your prayer? When you pray in your own words, who do you think is listening? Make a list of the names you recognize as referring to God, like "Creator," "Redeemer," "Lord," "Father." It can be long or short. Then zero in on the words or phrases that have the most significance for you. Which one comes closest to naming the God to whom you pray? Why does that name mean God for you?

2. Draw a timeline of your life, marking some of the most important events or transitions, such as marriage, illness, moving to another city—whatever had real significance for you. Pay attention to the memories and to the feelings they evoke. Be attentive to the presence of God in your life, both in the past and right now. Reflect on who God was for you at each of those points in your life. Has your image of God changed over the years? If so, how? Do you feel closer to God, or farther away?

3. Jesus is asking *you*: Who do you say that I am?

Who Are You for God?

Scripture: Luke 5:27–28

[Jesus] saw a tax collector named Levi sitting at the customs post. He said to him, "Follow me." And leaving everything behind, he got up and followed him.

What does "leaving everything" mean to older adults? What do we have to "leave behind"?

Perhaps we are being called to leave behind not our homes or families or professional responsibilities but whatever holds us back from a fuller and deeper relationship with God. It may be an attachment to something material. It may be our comfortable, usual way of doing certain things, or it may be a long-standing, deep-seated grievance we need to let go of.

It may be as simple as leaving behind what we were called to be in the past and embracing who we are now. For many people, it means making life-changing decisions, such as what to do in retirement; or whether to move from a house full of memories to an apartment or to assisted living; or how to be a caregiver for someone who is chronically or terminally ill.

All these transitions, even the painful ones, are calls to discipleship.

Who is a disciple? We often think first of the twelve apostles. On further reflection, we usually remember that the Gospels use the term "disciples" to mean a broader group of the followers of Jesus. There were the seventy-two whom Jesus sent out "in pairs to every town and place where he intended to visit" (Luke 10:1). There was Mary Magdalene, often called "the apostle to the apostles" because she was the first to bring them the news of the Resurrection. There were also the mostly unnamed women of Galilee who followed Jesus on his journeys. Mark says they "ministered to him" (15:41); somebody cooked the meals and did the laundry.

All these disciples had different gifts. Some served as advance men for Jesus, proclaiming the good news before him. Others used their humble, everyday skills to support his ministry.

How does discipleship change as we age? Many older adults are called upon to use different gifts from those that were most useful in raising their families or pursuing their careers. Some of the men and women discussed in the succeeding chapters illustrate how God calls us to different forms of discipleship in later years: Moses, for example, was called away from his pastoral life at age eighty to a leadership role he could not have imagined. Others, like Joseph, Miriam, or Simon's mother-in-law, were called to make use in later life of gifts they apparently had all along. John, "the beloved disciple," seems to have been still young when Jesus called him to care for Mary, but his story nevertheless resonates with older adults who are called to be caregivers, often for long periods of time.

PRAYER STARTERS

1. Can you name your gifts? What unique gifts has God given you?

   - Do you have the practical wisdom that comes from life experience?
   - Do you have the gift of faith and the desire to pray?
   - Do you have the gift of serving others, as a caregiver or a volunteer?
   - Do you have creative gifts: drawing or painting, photography, baking, gardening, playing the piano?
   - Do you have the gift of friendship? Of gratitude? Of patience? Of the ability to smile?
   - Which of these gifts is God calling you to use at this time in your life?

2. Pray with 1 Corinthians 12:4–11. Notice that St. Paul is talking about spiritual gifts. Which ones resonate with you? What about intellectual gifts, material gifts, creative gifts? There are different kinds of gifts but the same Spirit. What gifts has the Spirit given you?

3. Thank God for all your gifts, or for any one in particular that the Spirit called to your attention during this prayer.

4. Reread Luke 9:18–20, with which we began this chapter. Turn the question around: Ask God in prayer, "Lord, who do you say that I am?"

3

The Call to Recognize
What Is Possible: Anna

Scripture: Luke 2:22–24, 36–38

When the days were completed for their purification according to the law of Moses, they took him up to Jerusalem to present him to the Lord, just as it is written in the law of the Lord, "Every male that opens the womb shall be consecrated to the Lord," and to offer the sacrifice of "a pair of turtledoves or two young pigeons," in accordance with the dictate in the law of the Lord.

———

There was also a prophetess, Anna, the daughter of Phanuel, of the tribe of Asher. She was advanced in years, having lived seven years with her husband after her marriage, and then as a widow until she was eighty-four. She never left the temple, but worshiped night and day with fasting and prayer. And coming forward at that very time, she gave thanks to God and spoke about the child to all who were awaiting the redemption of Jerusalem.

Anna is part of the Christmas story. It's easy to overlook her among the many characters in Luke's infancy narrative because she has only a few verses, which are interrupted in the middle by the story of a male disciple who is given more space (Luke 2:22–35). But Anna's brief story presents a powerful role model for older adults.

Anna was eighty-four years old. That was an extraordinary age in first-century Palestine, when the average life expectancy was less than forty. In addition, she was widowed at a young age. That was nothing short of a calamity in a patriarchal society where women had no status apart from the men in their families. She spent the rest of her life in the temple, worshiping "night and day with fasting and prayer."

Then one day, Mary and Joseph brought the infant Jesus to the Temple, and Anna, a widow of advanced age with absolutely no status in the community, was given the grace to *recognize* him.

Anna was one of the first disciples. She was called to recognize the possibility of doing what must have seemed inconceivable: to break the silence imposed on women and speak about the grace she had been given. The eagerness with which she did so comes through in Luke's brief summary of her joyful proclamation: "She gave thanks to God and spoke about the child to all who were awaiting the redemption of Jerusalem."

The graces that Anna experienced were all the more extraordinary because she was a woman. Throughout his ministry, Jesus evidenced a countercultural attitude toward women, culminating when he commissioned Mary Magdalene to communicate the news of the Resurrection to the male disciples (John 20:17)—an event so extraordinary that they refused to believe her (Luke 24:10–11). Anna, a generation earlier, was one of the first women called to break boundaries. She recognized what was possible and answered the call with eagerness and joy.

It's worth noting that Anna was not unprepared for these graces. She had nurtured the gifts of prayer and deep contemplation during the long years she spent in the Temple. Then, all unasked for, very late in life, God gave her the gift of prophecy and called her to preach. She had different gifts, at different times in her life.

As we experience major changes in our lives—widowhood or retirement or responsibilities for aging parents—God may be calling us to new forms of discipleship and giving us the graces we need to answer the call.

PRAYER STARTERS

1. Imagine you are Anna, holding the infant Jesus in your arms, looking into his eyes. What do you see? How do you feel?

2. What are some of the special gifts God gives to us in later years? What are the obstacles or challenges that hinder us from using them?

3. Review the timeline you created in chapter 2. What gifts did God give you at earlier turning points in your life? What are the gifts you are aware of now? Ask for the grace to see all the possibilities.

4

The Call to Trust: Abram

Scripture: Genesis 12:1–5

The Lord said to Abram: Go forth from your land, your relatives, and from your father's house to a land that I will show you. I will make of you a great nation, and I will bless you; I will make your name great, so that you will be a blessing. I will bless those who bless you and curse those who curse you. All the families of the earth will find blessing in you. Abram went as the Lord directed him, and Lot went with him. Abram was seventy-five years old when he left Haran. Abram took his wife Sarai, his brother's son Lot, all the possessions that they had accumulated, and the persons they had acquired in Haran, and they set out for the land of Canaan.

Scripture scholars believe that Abram (whom God later renamed Abraham) lived around 1900 BC, almost four thousand years ago. People at that time lived their whole lives in their native villages. They had little idea of what life was like in the next valley, let alone twenty or fifty or a hundred miles away. They had no maps; they had no education; the world beyond them was a great mystery—a fearsome mystery.

We have no idea what life expectancy was twenty centuries before Christ, but it certainly wasn't long. Seventy-five was a great age.

And yet when Abram was seventy-five years old, God called him to leave behind everything he knew—his land, his relatives, his "father's house" and all that implied—and venture into the unknown, "to a land that I will show you."

And Abram went.

Most of us are not called to leave everything in God's service. But we are all called to trust. We all face the unknown in one form or another. Will I have enough money to last the rest of my life? Who will take care of me when I can no longer manage on my own?

PRAYER STARTERS

1. Are you facing a decision about moving? If so, how can Abram's call help you pray about the decision?

2. What are the uncertainties in your life? Can you pray for the grace to trust?

3. Pray with Genesis 22:1–13, where Abraham is again called upon to trust in God's promises even when God is telling him to sacrifice his only son. What do you think Abraham and Isaac talked about on the way home?

5

The Call to Stillness: Joseph

Scripture: Matthew 1:18–24

Now this is how the birth of Jesus Christ came about. When his mother Mary was betrothed to Joseph, but before they lived together, she was found with child through the holy Spirit. Joseph her husband, since he was a righteous man, yet unwilling to expose her to shame, decided to divorce her quietly. Such was his intention when, behold, the angel of the Lord appeared to him in a dream and said, "Joseph, son of David, do not be afraid to take Mary your wife into your home. For it is through the holy Spirit that this child has been conceived in her. She will bear a son and you are to name him Jesus, because he will save his people from their sins." All this took place to fulfill what the Lord had said through the prophet: "Behold, the virgin shall be with child and bear a son, and they shall name him Emmanuel," which means "God is with us." When Joseph awoke, he did as the angel of the Lord had commanded him and took his wife into his home.

Joseph's age is nowhere suggested in the Bible, but tradition depicts him as an older man. He is last mentioned in the Gospels on an occasion when Jesus was twelve years old (Luke 2:41–51), and his absence from both the marriage feast at Cana (John 2:1–12) and the Crucifixion suggests that he had died before the public ministry of Jesus began. An ancient tradition, generally accepted by Orthodox Christians but not by the Roman Catholic Church, depicts Joseph as a widower with children from his first marriage; hence the "brothers" of Jesus referred to at various points in the Gospels.

Whatever his age, God called Joseph in a way he had never imagined. When he contracted to marry the teenage Mary, he would probably have been looking forward to children: one could never have too many in the ancient world, where life expectancy was short and there was no social safety net for people who had no one to care for them in old age. Instead, God told him that his role was to be the guardian and protector of a son not his own—a son conceived by the Holy Spirit—and to live in a chaste relationship with his young bride.

As if this were not enough, this late call came to Joseph *in a dream*. Although Zechariah and Mary were expressly called by the angel Gabriel (Luke 1:5–20, 26–38), Joseph had no such tangible experience. His dream was a one-way conversation.

It was also in dreams that Joseph was later prompted to go to Egypt (Matthew 2:13–15) and still later to return to Israel (Matthew 2:19–22). Zechariah expressed disbelief and was punished for his doubt (Luke 1:18–20); Mary asked questions and was reassured (Luke 1:34–37). Joseph was given no such opportunity. He was called upon to obey unquestionably. And he did.

Nowhere in the Gospels is Joseph quoted as speaking a word—to God, to Mary, to the child Jesus, or to anyone else. Even when the anxious parents found Jesus in the Temple after three days of searching, it was Mary who did all the talking (Luke 2:46–51).

Joseph was silent. In the stillness, he heard God's call.

Joseph's silent acceptance of God's call could not have occurred without a deep inner stillness, the fruit of his prayer and openness to God.

I thought of Joseph during an eight-day silent retreat at a traditional retreat house. No one talked, but the retreat house staff always seemed to be bustling about: moving flower pots, opening and closing doors, doing various tasks. There was silence, but no stillness.

As we grow older, some of us are blessed with more free time and more opportunities to cultivate silence, and thus to grow into stillness.

PRAYER STARTERS

1. Take a walk in the woods or along a deserted beach, or anywhere you are unlikely to meet people or hear city noises. Listen to birds singing or waves rising and falling. Pause and feel the stillness.

2. If you are awake during the night, listen attentively to the sounds in your home. Use this moment to savor the stillness.

3. Ask Joseph about his dreams. Did he tell anyone about them? What was the reaction? Pray for the grace to share the stillness.

4. Pray with one of the following:

    Psalm 131

    LORD, my heart is not proud;
    nor are my eyes haughty.
    I do not busy myself with great matters,
    with things too sublime for me.
    Rather, I have stilled my soul,
    Like a weaned child to its mother,
    weaned is my soul.
    Israel, hope in the LORD,
    now and forever.

    Psalm 46:11, "Be still and know that I am God!"
    1 Kings 19:11–13, in which Elijah hears the voice of God in "a light silent sound."

6

The Call to Decide: Moses

Scripture: Exodus 3:10–14; 4:1, 10–17; 6:29–30; 7:6–7

Now, go! I am sending you to Pharaoh to bring my people, the Israelites, out of Egypt.

But Moses said to God, "Who am I that I should go to Pharaoh and bring the Israelites out of Egypt?" God answered: I will be with you; and this will be your sign that I have sent you. When you have brought the people out of Egypt, you will serve God at this mountain.

"But," said Moses to God, "if I go to the Israelites and say to them, 'The God of your ancestors has sent me to you,' and they ask me, 'What is his name?' what do I tell them?" God replied to Moses: I am who I am. Then he added: This is what you will tell the Israelites: I AM has sent me to you.

———

"But," objected Moses, "suppose they do not believe me or listen to me?"

———

Moses, however, said to the LORD, "If you please, my Lord, I have never been eloquent, neither in the past nor now that you have spoken to your servant; but I am slow of speech and tongue." The Lord said to him: Who gives one person speech? Who makes another mute or deaf, seeing or blind? Is it not I, the LORD? Now go, I will assist you in speaking and teach you what you are to say.

But he said, "If you please, my Lord, send someone else!" Then the LORD became angry with Moses and said: I know there is your brother, Aaron the Levite, who is a good speaker; even now he is on his way to meet you. When he sees you, he will truly be glad. You will speak to him and put the words in his mouth. I will assist both you and him in speaking and teach you both what you are to do. He will speak to the people for you: he will be your spokesman, and you will be as God to him. Take this staff in your hand; with it you are to perform the signs.

––––––

The LORD said to Moses: I am the LORD. Say to Pharaoh, king of Egypt, all that I tell you.

But Moses protested to the LORD, "Since I am a poor speaker, how is it possible that Pharaoh will listen to me?"

––––––

This, then, is what Moses and Aaron did. They did exactly as the LORD had commanded them. Moses was eighty years old, and Aaron eighty-three, when they spoke to Pharaoh.

Moses had already had an extremely eventful life. As an infant, he was saved from certain death by being floated down the Nile in a basket and then raised by Pharaoh's daughter as her own son (Exodus 2:1–10). He fled the court after killing an Egyptian who was abusing a Hebrew slave, and he settled down in Midian, where he married the daughter of the local priest and seems to have had a peaceful life tending his father-in-law's flocks (Exodus 2:11–15, 21; 3:1). At eighty years old—an advanced age in a primitive society—he probably had grandchildren and great-grandchildren, and looked forward to peacefully ending his days in the community that had welcomed him as a stranger and an outlaw. After "a long time passed" (Exodus 2:23), God suddenly called him to something he could scarcely comprehend: go to Pharaoh, and lead the enslaved Israelites to freedom.

Moses's reaction was to argue with God—at great length, as this abbreviated Scripture excerpt demonstrates (for the full dialogue, see Exodus 3:1–7:7) The word "but" appears repeatedly as Moses lists his excuses, one after another: he is nobody; the people will not believe he has been sent by God; he is not eloquent but "slow of speech and tongue"; and finally, "send someone else!" His resistance was so strong that God even became "angry" with him. Yet, in the end, he went. His subsequent adventures—the plagues, the Passover, the Exodus, the crossing of the Red Sea, receiving the Law directly from God, and wandering in the desert for many years on the way to the Promised Land—take up the next four books of the Hebrew Bible. Once Moses stopped saying "but"—stopped making excuses—God made him a leader.

As we age, many of us face life-changing decisions for which we have little preparation and conflicting feelings that tempt us to resist change.

Is retirement a call to do something new, such as volunteer service, deeper prayer, or creative activities? Or does it mean invisibility, loneliness, even worthlessness?

Is downsizing (for example, to a smaller house) a call to move away from attachment to material things and focus on what really matters? Or is it too painful to consider?

Is caregiving for a parent or spouse a call to understand suffering in a new way? Or does it seem like an unbearable burden?

It isn't always easy to hear a call to discipleship in situations such as these. It can be quite easy to make excuses: BUT I'm too old; BUT it's too much to ask; BUT I don't have the physical or emotional strength for this.

There is clearly more to decisions of this kind than listing the "buts." A call from God deserves prayerful consideration. The Spiritual Exercises of St. Ignatius devote considerable attention to decision making. In simplified form, there are two basic approaches:

1. Combine prayer with reasoning:

   - Define the question.
   - Strive to be as detached as possible without assuming the result you prefer.
   - Ask God to move your will toward what pleases him.
   - List and rationally consider the advantages and disadvantages of each option.
   - Make a decision based on what seems most reasonable.
   - Bring the decision to prayer and ask God to receive and confirm it.

2. Combine prayer with discernment of your deepest feelings, using questions such as the following:

   - What is drawing me toward God?
   - What is drawing me away from God?
   - What leads me to a loving relationship with others?
   - What reflects my selfish instincts?
   - What leads to feelings of peace?
   - What causes turmoil and anxiety?

PRAYER STARTERS

1. Lord, you want me to do WHAT?! But I'm too old. You want me to step outside my comfort zone and go where the Spirit leads me? Lord, I'm willing to try. BUT I can't do it alone! Give me the grace to trust you!

2. Challenge yourself to pray about how God is calling you at this stage of your life and to ask for the grace to stop making excuses.

3. When have you said "BUT . . ." to God? Can you rephrase it as a prayer for help in overcoming whatever is holding you back?

7

The Call to Humility:
Naaman the Syrian

Scripture: 2 Kings 5:1–14

Naaman, the army commander of the king of Aram, was highly esteemed and respected by his master, for through him the LORD had brought victory to Aram. But valiant as he was, the man was a leper.

Now the Arameans had captured from the land of Israel in a raid a little girl, who became the servant of Naaman's wife. She said to her mistress, "If only my master would present himself to the prophet in Samaria! He would cure him of his leprosy." Naaman went and told his master, "This is what the girl from the land of Israel said." The king of Aram said, "Go. I will send along a letter to the king of Israel." So Naaman set out, taking along ten silver talents, six thousand gold pieces, and ten festal garments. He brought the king of Israel the letter, which read: "With this letter I am sending my servant Naaman to you, that you may cure him of his leprosy." When he read the letter, the king of Israel tore his garments and exclaimed: "Am I a god with power over life and death, that this man should send someone for me to cure him of leprosy? Take note! You can see he is only looking for a quarrel with me!"

When Elisha, the man of God, heard that the king of Israel had torn his garments, he sent word to the king: "Why have you torn your garments? Let him come to me and find out that there is a prophet in Israel." Naaman came with his horses and chariot and stopped at the door of Elisha's house. Elisha sent him the message: "Go and wash seven times in the Jordan, and your flesh will heal, and you will be clean." But Naaman went away angry, saying, "I thought that he would surely come out to me and stand there to call on the name of the LORD his God, and would move his hand over the place, and thus cure the leprous spot. Are not the rivers of Damascus, the Abana and the Pharpar, better than all the waters of Israel? Could I not wash in them and be cleansed?" With this, he turned about in anger and left.

But his servants came up and reasoned with him: "My father, if the prophet told you to do something extraordinary, would you not do it? All the more since he told you, 'Wash, and be clean'?" So Naaman went down and plunged into the Jordan seven times, according to the word of the man of God. His flesh became again like the flesh of a little child, and he was clean.

Namaan came to Elisha with his horses and chariots, evidently expecting the prophet to perform some kind of elaborate rite to cure him. When Elisha didn't even come out to meet him, but sent word that he should go and wash seven times in the Jordan River, Namaan was furious. Had he made this arduous journey, endured the rage of the king of Israel, only to be humiliated in front of all his retinue?

Fortunately, his servants reasoned with him. They said, "Father, if the prophet told you to do something extraordinary, would you not do it?" So Namaan did as the prophet instructed him, and he was cured.

The servants' question is every bit as relevant to us. If the Lord Jesus told us to do something extraordinary, would we not do it?

Of course we would.

So how will we respond if he asks us to spend more time in prayer, contemplation, discernment?

Some of us experienced such a call when directed to "shelter in place" during the peak of the COVID-19 pandemic. None of us knows when such a situation may recur, or for how long. When we are deprived of normal activities such as going to work, volunteering, or socializing with friends, we may be able to find more time for prayer. It can be humbling to realize that prayer is the only thing God is asking of us right now.

In more normal times, it can be difficult to accept the idea that God may be calling us, not to great deeds, but to humble ones. The newly retired, for example, may want to volunteer in any number of active causes and yet discern a call to serve in less visible ways. Naaman's example—coming reluctantly to humility and trust—may illuminate the process.

PRAYER STARTERS

1. Pray with John 15:16a: "It was not you who chose me, but I who chose you and appointed you to go and bear fruit that will remain."
2. How is God calling you at the present time? What, if any, resistance do you sense within yourself? Then listen to Namaan's servants.
3. How can you spend more "quality time" with God?

8

The Call to Adapt to Radical Change: Paul

Scripture: Acts 28:30–31

He remained for two full years in his lodgings. He received all who came to him, and with complete assurance and without hindrance he proclaimed the kingdom of God and taught about the Lord Jesus Christ.

Paul had an extraordinarily active life. It's exhausting just to read about his missionary journeys: the many times he was shipwrecked, persecuted, imprisoned, and beaten. Finally, he was accused of various crimes by the Jewish authorities and exercised his right as a Roman citizen to appeal his case to Caesar (Acts 25:11). When he got to Rome, after another adventurous journey (Acts 27:1–28:14), he was placed under house arrest, with a soldier to guard him (Acts 28:16).

Imagine how he felt. After spending most of his adult life traveling around the whole Mediterranean world, preaching and teaching and arguing, and later baptizing and founding churches, suddenly he found himself confined to a rented lodging, all alone except for a guard, in a place where the new movement of Christianity was viewed with suspicion. What did he do?

He found a new way of exercising discipleship. Instead of a life of constant motion, he discerned a call to greater stability. Instead of seeking out and preaching to large groups, he "received all who came to him." He responded to a call to radical change.

With the help of the Holy Spirit, so can we. Retirement, the empty-nest experience, widowhood—all these states of life might call for the kind of radical change that Paul experienced. Can we let go of our assumptions about how God may be calling us?

PRAYER STARTERS

1. Imagine yourself being received by Paul at his Roman lodgings. What is it like? What is he like? What advice do you seek from him?

2. If you have recently experienced a major life transition, make an inventory of the ways your life is different now—for example, in daily routines, in feelings, in opportunities. Where do you sense the presence of the Holy Spirit?

3. How do you put limits on God's grace? Ask Paul to show you how to be open to change.

9

The Call to Serve:
Simon's Mother-in-Law

Scripture: Mark 1:29–31

On leaving the synagogue [Jesus] entered the house of
Simon and Andrew with James and John. Simon's mother-
in-law lay sick with a fever. They immediately told him
about her. He approached, grasped her hand, and helped
her up. Then the fever left her and she waited on them.

Jesus must surely have been looking forward to a peaceful
Sabbath meal at Simon Peter's house, after teaching in the
synagogue, curing a demoniac, and enduring the commotion
that ensued (Mark 1:21–28). Instead, he had barely crossed
the threshold when he was called to the bedside of a sick
woman. He cured her without a word, and her immediate
response was to "wait on" Jesus and all his company.

Who was this nameless woman, who is given only two
sentences in Mark's Gospel? She was certainly "old" by
first-century standards, given that she had a married

daughter. The all-encompassing term "fever" often meant a life-threatening illness or even demonic possession. (In another version of this event, Luke 4:39, Jesus "rebuked" the fever.) Nevertheless, in the multigenerational households of the time, this woman would still have had major responsibilities, including hospitality to guests.

Sick as she was, how could she get up and dress and greet visitors? Worse, Jesus wasn't alone; he brought James and John and who knows how many others with him. How could she trust anyone else—her daughters, her daughters-in-law, or any of the other women of the household? Yet she had no strength. How frustrated she must have felt in her weakness, pain, and anxiety.

Then "they" (who are "they"?) "told him about her." How did she feel when Jesus—perhaps accompanied by "them"—came into her private space? Surprised? Embarrassed? Hopeful? "They told him about her." What had anybody told *her* about *him*?

Then, suddenly, he cured her. How did she feel when the illness left her all at once? Her joy and gratitude were so full that she "waited on them." She expressed her feelings with loving, personal service.

The ways of serving others are beyond numbering. Older adults who do volunteer work among the poor and the marginalized, serve as caregivers for grandchildren or disabled family members, give financial support, or simply pray fervently for all those in need—all these people have discovered how God is calling them to serve in their particular circumstances. The story of Simon's mother-in-law challenges us to make it more personal, to "wait on" those we serve with patience and joy.

PRAYER STARTERS

1. How might Simon's mother-in-law help us imagine what it is like to meet Jesus?

2. Ask yourself: How am I called to "wait on" Jesus? Who in my life needs the kind of loving personal service that Simon's mother-in-law gave him?

10

The Call to Caregiving: John

Scripture: John 19:25–27

Standing by the cross of Jesus were his mother and his mother's sister, Mary the wife of Clopas, and Mary of Magdala. When Jesus saw his mother and the disciple there whom he loved, he said to his mother, "Woman, behold, your son." Then he said to the disciple, "Behold, your mother." And from that hour the disciple took her into his home.

Scripture scholars, as well as ancient tradition, identify the anonymous "disciple . . . whom [Jesus] loved" as John, who is recognized as the author of the Gospel bearing his name, as well as three epistles and the book of Revelation. He is believed to have been the youngest of the twelve apostles, and in religious art he is often depicted as beardless, which in ancient times would have been unusual for an adult male. He was also the only one of the male disciples who remained at the foot of the cross while the others fled in fear.

Youth, closeness to Jesus, and being there in a time of disaster—all good qualities in a prospective caregiver. Jesus, breathing with difficulty and speaking with painful effort, did not spend time or energy explaining to John that caring for Mary was his call, one that might extend for many years. Nor did he wait for John to indicate his acceptance.

How did John feel about this new call? He might have remembered Jesus saying, at the Last Supper, "It was not you who chose me, but I who chose you and appointed you to go and bear fruit that will remain, so that whatever you ask the Father in my name he may give you" (John 15:16).

Those of us much older than John who may be cast in the role of caregiver for a disabled spouse or parent may have difficulty seeing it as a call. Women of the "sandwich generation" who have responsibilities for both children and parents may feel unfairly put upon, angry, depressed: We didn't *choose* this life!

Thinking of it as a call may not be easy, if there is no opportunity to say no. John, despite his youth, may serve as a role model for the acceptance of such a call.

Caregiving in twenty-first-century America is often a thankless task. Some financial assistance is available from Medicaid or private insurance for disabled people confined to nursing homes, but help in caring for them at home is often more difficult to come by. Conditions in some nursing homes are appalling, and the failure of regulatory agencies to stop abuses became glaringly evident when the COVID-19 virus attacked the most vulnerable residents in facilities that were totally unprepared to protect them. The warehousing of the sick and dying in such institutions, as well as the increasing support for physician-assisted suicide (currently legal in nine states), reflect an absence of appreciation—if not outright contempt—for the dignity of the aged and infirm. At the opposite extreme, people with terminal illnesses are sometimes subjected to interventions that do little except to prolong their suffering without hope of a cure when hospice care would be a more compassionate alternative. To complete the picture, home health aides whose full-time job is caring for the disabled are often paid little more than the minimum wage, and during the height of the COVID-19 pandemic had great difficulty obtaining protective equipment, despite the dangers involved in serving several patients in their respective homes.

Against this background, it may be less difficult to see caregiving as a call, however unwelcome, and pray for the grace to live it.

PRAYER STARTERS

1. If you are a caregiver, pray to St. John for the grace to live your call with love and trust.
2. Pray with John 15:16. What has God chosen you for?
3. What can we do to promote awareness of the dignity of the aging, the disabled, the dying, and those who care for them?

11

The Call to Accept Being Served: Naomi * Peter

Scripture: Ruth 1:6–21

[Naomi's family emigrated from Bethlehem to Moab; after a number of years, her husband and both her sons died. Ruth 1:1–5]

[Naomi] and her daughters-in-law then prepared to go back from the plateau of Moab because word had reached her there that the LORD had seen to his people's needs and given them food. She and her two daughters-in-law left the place where they had been living. On the road back to the land of Judah, Naomi said to her daughters-in-law, "Go back, each of you to your mother's house. . . . [M]y lot is too bitter for you, because the LORD has extended his hand against me." . . .

But Ruth said, "Do not press me to go back and abandon you! Wherever you go I will go, wherever you lodge I will lodge. Your people shall be my people and your God, my God. Where you die I will die, and there be buried. May the LORD do thus to me, and more, if even death separates me from you!" Naomi then ceased to urge her, for she saw she was determined to go with her. So they went on together until they reached Bethlehem. On their arrival there, the whole town was excited about them, and the women asked: "Can this be Naomi?" But she said to them, "Do not call me Naomi ['Sweet']. Call me Mara ['Bitter'], for the Almighty has made my life very bitter. I went away full, but the LORD has brought me back empty. Why should you call me 'Sweet,' since the LORD has brought me to trial, and the Almighty has pronounced evil sentence on me."

Naomi's situation was all too familiar in ancient times: a widow with no sons or other male relatives to provide for her, facing grinding poverty. Her bleak prospects were rendered more desperate by the fact that she was an immigrant. She could not expect charity from her Moabite neighbors in a land where she had no relatives. Her one hope was to return to her own land, where distant relatives might offer some form of help, if only in permission to glean the leftovers from what promised to be an abundant harvest.

Naomi's Moabite daughters-in-law were not much better off, as childless widows. For them at least, remaining in their own land might present the possibility of remarriage. Naomi clearly understood this when she urged them to stay behind. She was vocal in her bitterness at the trials God had sent her at this time in her life. There may be just a hint of self-pity in the repetition of this lament.

Ruth, however, would have none of it. She saw her duty as taking care of her mother-in-law, no matter what. Naomi reluctantly acceded to Ruth's determination, although she was still bitter when they arrived in Bethlehem. Only very slowly did she begin to hope as Ruth began to support them both, first by retrieving the leftovers from the newly harvested fields (Ruth 2:1–17), and eventually by marrying one of Naomi's distant relatives (Ruth 4:9–17).

In ancient societies, mothers-in-law had great authority over their sons' wives, who joined their households upon marriage and were part of a structure of rank that included the daughters, sisters, and servants of the matriarch. Thus, Naomi's unwillingness to be cared for by her sons' widows was so strong that she was even prepared to undertake the dangerous journey to Bethlehem alone.

It isn't difficult to understand Naomi's bitterness in these circumstances. It can resonate with anyone who has experienced the shock, anger, and pain of losing a spouse. Whether they need financial help or help with daily living, widows and widowers often must rely on their adult children in unexpected ways. It's not easy to accept help as we age. When children take on the care and support of their parents, the role reversal can be stressful for both. People who have spent their adult lives caring for others—raising their families or performing various kinds of service in their careers or volunteer work—find this particularly difficult.

Others who may identify with Naomi include people who have been "downsized" from rewarding work in middle age or later. Age discrimination may be illegal, but that does not prevent it from happening. Job seekers in their fifties and sixties, no matter how excellent their credentials, often find that they must settle for lower-paying jobs, perhaps in the "gig economy," or depend on their families for support. Even where, as in Naomi's case, a parent has no choice but to accept support from a younger person, it can be a blow to pride, a humiliation for which he or she is not prepared.

PRAYER STARTERS

1. What do you need help with? Pray for the grace to be honest.

2. Can you ask for help when you need it? What sometimes gets in your way of asking for help? Pray for the grace to be humble.

3. How do you respond to unsolicited offers of help? Pray for the grace to be grateful, even if you don't really need the help that is offered.

4. Try to put yourself in the shoes of the person offering help. How would you want your offer to be received?

Peter

Scripture: John 13:1–9

Before the feast of Passover, Jesus knew that his hour had come to pass from this world to the Father. He loved his own in the world and he loved them to the end. The devil had already induced Judas, son of Simon the Iscariot, to hand him over. So, during supper, fully aware that the Father had put everything into his power and that he had come from God and was returning to God, he rose from supper and took off his outer garments. He took a towel and tied it around his waist. Then he poured water into a basin and began to wash the disciples' feet and dry them with the towel around his waist. He came to Simon Peter, who said to him, "Master, are you going to wash my feet?" Jesus answered and said to him, "What I am doing, you do not understand now, but you will understand later." Peter said to him, "You will never wash my feet." Jesus answered him, "Unless I wash you, you will have no inheritance with me." Simon Peter said to him, "Master, then not only my feet, but my hands and head as well."

This passage is read every year on Holy Thursday, and in most Roman Catholic and some Protestant parishes it is followed by the celebrant washing the feet of twelve people, usually on chairs placed directly in front of the altar, for all to see. In many parishes, a staff person or liturgy committee chair has arranged in advance with twelve individuals to represent the congregation; in others, volunteers are asked for, and anyone may come forward. When this custom first came into common use in Roman Catholic parishes following the Second Vatican Council, there was some debate about how representative the twelve people should be. Some pastors were of the view that these individuals represented the twelve apostles, and that therefore only males should have their feet washed. Others took the broader view that this story was about service, and that the priest's action represented the service Jesus enjoined upon his disciples in the succeeding verses (John 13:12–17). It can be a challenge for many of us to imagine ourselves performing this kind of service: washing the dirty feet of a stranger.

But there is another side of this story, often overlooked: the experience of being served by Jesus.

Peter's humility and impulsive expression of love appear in a number of places in the Gospels. When called by Jesus after a miraculous catch of fish, his response was "Depart from me, Lord, for I am a sinful man" (Luke 5:4–8). At the Transfiguration, he was eager to build tabernacles for Jesus, Moses, and Elijah (Matthew 17:1–8). And when Jesus was seized in the Garden of Gethsemane, he was ready to fight, cutting off a man's ear (John 18:10). Here, overwhelmed with the magnitude of what Jesus is doing, he blurts out that he wants no part of it; then he accepts with even more vehemence when he understands the full profundity of the situation: he can have no part in Jesus if he does not allow Jesus to serve him!

PRAYER STARTERS

Imagine Jesus washing your feet. How do you feel? What do you say to him?

12

The Call to Generosity:
Lydia * Widow of Zarephath

Scripture: Acts 16:13–15

On the sabbath we went outside the city gate along the river where we thought there would be a place of prayer. We sat and spoke with the women who had gathered there. One of them, a woman named Lydia, a dealer in purple cloth, from the city of Thyatira, a worshiper of God, listened, and the Lord opened her heart to pay attention to what Paul was saying. After she and her household had been baptized, she offered us an invitation, "If you consider me a believer in the Lord, come and stay at my home," and she prevailed on us.

Lydia's age is not given, but we can infer from her status as a successful businesswoman with a large household that she was not young. She was also wealthy, as purple cloth was an expensive luxury in the ancient world. As a "worshiper of God," she was a Gentile who accepted Jewish monotheism but was not bound by Jewish law. In other words, she was ready to hear about a Messiah who was savior to Jews and Gentiles alike.

She may not have been ready for the way the message came. A group of women, most likely Lydia's relatives and servants, was gathered, probably for prayer, when two or more men abruptly appeared and sat down among them. In Philippi, a Roman colony and a city of some size, the sexes may not have been as rigidly separated as in some other parts of the ancient world, but it was nevertheless not usual for unrelated men and women to mingle in public. But Paul began immediately to preach, probably at characteristic length. And Lydia *listened*.

That is how "the Lord opened her heart to pay attention to what Paul was saying." She listened to a strange man, in unusual circumstances, and immediately understood that God speaks to us in unexpected ways. She seems to have been baptized without delay, along with her whole household.

As a way of living the new message of love, Lydia's immediate reaction was to offer hospitality to Paul and his companions. Although Paul plied his trade of tent making whenever he could, most of his time was spent traveling, with all the hazards and delays that were normal in the first century. He depended to a great extent on the kindness of believers in the cities and towns he visited. Lydia understood this, and "prevailed" upon them, suggesting some reluctance on Paul's part and a strong sense of urgency on Lydia's part.

Lydia is not mentioned again in the Bible, but these few verses present an eloquent picture of a later-life conversion experience. Once the Lord "opened her heart," she found a new way of using her considerable resources to support Paul's ministry and, through him, the spread of the gospel. She is a good role model for many of us who are not ourselves called to undertake missionary activity but who can support and sustain others on the spiritual journey.

It is significant that what Lydia offered to Paul and his companions was not money but hospitality. In the twenty-first century, it's easy enough to respond to the needs of others by writing a check. Whether small or large, cash contributions sustain the life-saving mission of many organizations that help the poorest of the poor. But if we truly open our hearts, as Lydia did, we may be moved to do more.

Generosity can take many forms. Lydia had a large enough household to offer room and board to the travelers. Those of us who live in one-family homes or small city apartments do not. But we can welcome new neighbors with genuine warmth and offers of help; we can assist those who serve the homeless in various ways; we can contribute canned goods and used clothing to food pantries and organizations that serve the poor; we can reach out to neighbors who may be housebound or lonely. Above all, we can cultivate an attitude of giving and make an effort to notice the opportunities that present themselves.

PRAYER STARTERS

1. God speaks to us in many ways, sometimes through the voices we least expect to hear. Are you listening?
2. Pray for the grace to develop an attitude of giving.
3. Ask God to open your heart to the needs of those around you, and pray for the grace to be generous with your resources of time, energy, and material things, whatever their extent.

The Widow of Zarephath

Scripture: 1 Kings 17:8–16

So the word of the Lord came to [Elijah]: Arise, go to Zarephath of Sidon and stay there. I have commanded a widow there to feed you. He arose and went to Zarephath. When he arrived at the entrance of the city, a widow was there gathering sticks; he called out to her, "Please bring me a small cupful of water to drink." She left to get it, and he called out after her, "Please bring along a crust of bread." She said, "As the LORD, your God, lives, I have nothing baked; there is only a handful of flour in my jar and a little oil in my jug. Just now I was collecting a few sticks, to go in and prepare something for myself and my son; when we have eaten it, we shall die." Elijah said to her, "Do not be afraid. Go and do as you have said. But first make me a little cake and bring it to me. Afterwards you can prepare something for yourself and your son. For the LORD, the God of Israel, says: The jar of flour shall not go empty, nor the jug of oil run dry, until the day when the LORD sends rain upon the earth." She left and did as Elijah had said. She had enough to eat for a long time—he and she and her household. The jar of flour did not go empty, nor the jug of oil run dry, according to the word of the LORD spoken through Elijah.

Unlike Lydia, the widow of Zarephath was poor, to the point of starvation. She was called to give, not out of abundance, but out of her need, her very substance. She was not only starving but despairing as she started to prepare what she expected would be her last meal.

I admit that I find it very difficult to enter the feelings of this woman, because I have never faced anything even remotely like the starvation she experienced. Even during World War II, when food rationing was in effect (there were little red tokens for meat, and blue ones for other foodstuffs, issued according to family size), my family lacked luxuries, but we always had enough to eat.

Privileged as I have been—and I do recognize that it is a privilege never to have to worry where the next meal is coming from—I have always been struck by the generosity of the poor.

When I volunteered as an English teacher at an immigrant services center, most of my students were older, some retired from hard work, others serving as full-time caretakers for grandchildren. Most were Chinese, and all were poor. They expressed their gratitude for the classes with a stream of small gifts: Asian pears and persimmons in season, eggplant and fresh ginger with instructions on how to cook it, and a lifetime supply of tea. Most semesters there were one or two students from other parts of the world, who were welcomed and encouraged. A woman from Haiti arrived after one of the many upheavals of that island nation. She had planned to stay with her mother and sister but found they were living in a small apartment shared by eleven people, so she moved among several temporary accommodations while trying desperately to find a way to reunite her family. Meanwhile, the Chinese ladies had somehow found out when my birthday was and planned a festive lunch at a local dim sum restaurant. On the day of the event, the Haitian student came to meet me in the office before class. She said: "I have nothing to give you, but I offered my rosary for you this morning." Nothing to give? This happened eight years ago, and I still feel blessed by her gift.

The widow of Zarephath responded unhesitatingly after Elijah explained God's promise and placed his need ahead of her own. What can we learn from her example?

PRAYER STARTERS

1. Can you imagine yourself in the position of the widow? What does it feel like to be starving?

2. Where did she find the strength to share the little she had?

3. What do you spend your food budget on? Are there luxuries you might be able to eliminate, in solidarity with the poor?

4. How can you increase your giving: material things, prayer, love?

13

The Call to Gratitude: The Tenth Leper

Scripture: Luke 17:11–19

As he continued his journey to Jerusalem, he traveled through Samaria and Galilee. As he was entering a village, ten lepers met [him]. They stood at a distance from him and raised their voice, saying, "Jesus, Master! Have pity on us!" And when he saw them, he said, "Go show yourselves to the priests." As they were going they were cleansed. And one of them, realizing he had been healed, returned, glorifying God in a loud voice; and he fell at the feet of Jesus and thanked him. He was a Samaritan. Jesus said in reply, "Ten were cleansed, were they not? Where are the other nine? Has none but this foreigner returned to give thanks to God?" Then he said to him, "Stand up and go; your faith has saved you."

Whatever their ages, these ten had a very short life expectancy. Leprosy was the most feared disease of the ancient world—incurable, contagious, and the cause of an agonizing death. A whole chapter of the Mosaic Law as explained in the book of Leviticus describes the detailed examinations to be conducted by the priests and the penalties imposed on those who were diagnosed with this dread disease. For example:

> The garments of one afflicted with a scaly infection shall be rent and the hair disheveled, and the mustache covered. The individual shall cry out, "Unclean, unclean!" As long as the infection is present, the person shall be unclean. Being unclean, that individual shall dwell apart, taking up residence outside the camp. (Leviticus 13:45–46)

Life, in short, was a living hell for those so afflicted. It is no surprise, then, that any who had heard of Jesus sought him out and begged for his healing power. What is surprising—astonishing, really—is that nine of the ten simply went on their way, with no gratitude: no words of thanks, not even any acknowledgment that they were healed or that Jesus had anything to do with it. It is surely one of the most glaring examples of ingratitude in the entire Bible.

St. Ignatius of Loyola thought ingratitude was the deadliest of all sins and the source of all others. Gratitude is a recurring theme in the Spiritual Exercises, as in this brief invitation to prayer:

> I beg for the gift of an intimate knowledge of all the goods which God lovingly shares with me. Filled with gratitude, I want to be empowered to respond just as totally in

my love and service. [Spiritual Exercises, § 233, Fleming translation]

Ignatius's insight is that we should ask God to show us what to be thankful for. Even gratitude to God is God's gift! The daily Examen—the prayer that Ignatius thought so important it should not be omitted even when there was no time for anything else—begins with thanksgiving for all the graces of the preceding day, large and small, temporary and permanent, the answers to our prayers and the things we take for granted.

For the aging, gratitude can be both easier and more difficult. It is often easier, as we look back, to see the grace in events and circumstances that we may not have appreciated at the time. However, some of the losses and sufferings we experience in the later years may dominate our consciousness in ways that make it difficult to focus on what we're grateful for. In short, it may take a little more effort to say a sincere prayer of thanksgiving. Blessed Titus Brandsma (1881–1942), in a poem written shortly before his execution at the Dachau concentration camp, thanked God for the silence that made him feel closer to Jesus:

Leave me here freely all alone,
In cell where never sunlight shone.
Should no one ever speak to me,
This golden silence makes me free!

The ingratitude of nine lepers is the opposite extreme of the heroism of a martyr. Most of us are likely to fall somewhere in between, as did the tenth leper. In his case, the impulse to thank God came with the *realization* that he had been cured. Reflecting on our own gifts may lead to a deeper realization of what to be grateful for.

PRAYER STARTERS

1. Review the preceding day, focusing on all the small details beginning with the moment you awoke. Where did you experience God's gifts? Thank God for each of them.
2. Have you ever taken God's gifts for granted? Thank God for all your more permanent gifts.
3. Imagine the joy of the tenth leper. Have you ever experienced such joy? Thank God for it.
4. Record in your spiritual journal some of the gifts, temporary and permanent, that you have identified. Return to this record whenever you have difficulty with a prayer of thanksgiving.

14

The Call to Creativity: Miriam

Scripture: Exodus 15:19–21

When Pharaoh's horses and chariots and horsemen entered the sea, the LORD made the waters of the sea flow back upon them, though the Israelites walked on dry land through the midst of the sea. Then the prophet Miriam, Aaron's sister, took a tambourine in her hand, while all the women went out after her with tambourines, dancing; and she responded to them:

> Sing to the LORD, for he is gloriously triumphant;
> horse and chariot he has cast into the sea.

Miriam was likely older than Moses, because she is usually identified as the sister who observed the infant Moses being placed in a basket on the river (Exodus 2:4). Whatever her years, she was advanced in age by the standards of the time. Some Scripture scholars believe the verse she sang was a kind of antiphon, repeated at intervals in the hymn set out in Exodus 15:1–18. Others credit her with both the words and the music of the entire song. Whatever the extent of her gifts,

God called her to use her talents for singing and dancing to express gratitude for the miracle of deliverance. The whole body of Israelites joined in.

After a monumental event that could hardly be described in words, Miriam received a once-in-a-lifetime call to use her special gifts to express the unbounded, overflowing joy of the entire community. She may well have developed those gifts in the context of community worship during the exile in Egypt. Now she was called upon to use them to glorify God in a completely new situation.

Earning a living and raising a family often leave little time to enjoy or develop some of the gifts that aren't directly related to our day-to-day obligations. There isn't time to play a musical instrument when one is working long hours, and it's not easy to paint or sculpt or write poetry with growing children in the house. But the gifts that haven't been used in a long time are still there. Many people who are retired or free of family obligations have the opportunity to nourish their creativity—or perhaps to discover creative gifts they never knew they had. Like Miriam, we might discover times and places to use our creative gifts that we never dreamed of—provided we are open to God's call.

If you use your unique gifts for the love of God, you are a disciple, as much as any missionary.

PRAYER STARTERS

1. Consider some of the following possibilities:

   Can you pray with music? Lift your voice in song? Play familiar hymns on the piano?

   Can you pray with art? Study a famous religious painting in a nearby museum or a book of religious art. Does it illuminate for you the Gospel story or other event depicted? Do you see the event the way the artist saw it, or differently?

   Can you add pencil sketches, or abstract designs, to the words in your journal?

   Do you like photography, woodworking, gardening, baking, arranging flowers, embroidery?

   How do these activities express the love of God?

2. Take a camera (or a smartphone) on a walk in the city or in the woods. Look around you, in front of you, and behind you, and photograph what you see. How does the camera change the way you see the details of creation?

3. Pray Psalm 150:

   > Hallelujah!
   > Praise God in his holy sanctuary;
   > give praise in the mighty dome of heaven.
   > Give praise for his mighty deeds,
   > praise him for his great majesty.
   > Give praise with blasts upon the horn
   > praise him with harp and lyre.
   > Give praise with tambourines and dance,

praise him with strings and pipes.
Give praise with crashing cymbals,
praise him with sounding cymbals.
Let everything that has breath
give praise to the LORD!
Hallelujah!

Add your own list of ways that you can praise God today.

15

The Call to Rejoice: Elizabeth

Scripture: Luke 1:36–45

"And behold, Elizabeth, your relative, has also conceived a son in her old age, and this is the sixth month for her who was called barren, for nothing will be impossible for God." Mary said, "Behold, I am the handmaid of the Lord. May it be done to me according to your word." Then the angel departed from her. During those days Mary set out and traveled to the hill country in haste to a town of Judah, where she entered the house of Zechariah and greeted Elizabeth. When Elizabeth heard Mary's greeting, the infant leaped in her womb, and Elizabeth, filled with the holy Spirit, cried out in a loud voice and said, "Most blessed are you among women, and blessed is the fruit of your womb. And how does this happen to me, that the mother of my Lord should come to me? For at the moment the sound of your greeting reached my ears, the infant in the womb leaped for joy. Blessed are you who believed that what was spoken to you by the Lord would be fulfilled."

"Old age" in first-century Palestine probably meant about forty—old for a first pregnancy even in our own times and probably considered impossible in those days. "Barren" was a stigma in an agrarian society that placed tremendous value on procreation. Childless at this advanced age, Elizabeth was disgraced, scorned, perhaps pitied.

Several months earlier, Elizabeth's husband, Zechariah, had been told by the angel Gabriel that his wife would bear a son, who would be the forerunner of the Messiah (Luke 1:8–17). Zechariah doubted this astonishing news and was punished for his lack of faith (Luke 1:18–20). Elizabeth, however, appears to have had no such doubts, as her joyful greeting to Mary shows. Although Luke tells us nothing more of Elizabeth's story, it seems clear that she had a good understanding of how God was at work in the world, in Mary's life, and in her own. Like Abram before her and Anna afterward, she had a life-changing call at an age when she never could have imagined such a thing—and she rejoiced.

When Mary arrived, Elizabeth already knew all about the child her cousin carried (Luke 1:41–45). It therefore seems reasonable to suppose that she too had a vision, whether in a dream like Joseph (Matthew 1:18–24) or by a visit from the angel Gabriel like Zechariah and Mary (Luke 1:10–20, 26–38).

Perhaps she could have described it this way:

He came when I was working in the garden.
It was a bright day; I squinted to see him in the
       brightness.
He said: When your husband Zechariah returns from his
       priestly duty,
you will conceive and bear a son. (I dared not breathe.)
He said: You must name him John.
He will be called by God to announce the coming of the
       Messiah. (I drew a deep breath.)
He said: Zechariah will be mute for a time because he
       doubted.
(I smiled at this, knowing how stubborn Zechariah
       can be.)
He said: The Messiah will be born of your young
       cousin Mary.
She will come to you in the spring.
She will need your advice and comfort as she deals with
       her unexpected pregnancy.
I said: I will welcome her with joy.
He smiled and was gone. The brightness lingered.

—Barbara Lee

PRAYER STARTERS

1. Where have you experienced joy today? Record it in your spiritual journal and reread it when you are feeling sad or negative.

2. Reflect on an event in your life that made you joyful. Savor it and thank God for it.

3. How can you bring joy into the lives of others? What can you do to comfort someone who is sick or grieving? Can you listen patiently to someone who talks too much?

16

The Call to Forgiveness:
The Father of Two Sons

Scripture: Luke 15:11–32

Then he said, "A man had two sons, and the younger son said to his father, 'Father, give me the share of your estate that should come to me.' So the father divided the property between them. After a few days, the younger son collected all his belongings and set off to a distant country where he squandered his inheritance on a life of dissipation. When he had freely spent everything, a severe famine struck that country, and he found himself in dire need. So he hired himself out to one of the local citizens who sent him to his farm to tend the swine. And he longed to eat his fill of the pods on which the swine fed, but nobody gave him any. Coming to his senses he thought, 'How many of my father's hired workers have more than enough food to eat, but here am I, dying from hunger. I shall get up and go to my father and I shall say to him, "Father, I have sinned against heaven and against you. I no longer deserve to be called your son; treat me as you would treat one of

your hired workers.'" So he got up and went back to his
father. While he was still a long way off, his father caught
sight of him, and was filled with compassion. He ran to
his son, embraced him and kissed him. His son said to
him, 'Father, I have sinned against heaven and against you;
I no longer deserve to be called your son.' But his father
ordered his servants, 'Quickly bring the finest robe and put
it on him; put a ring on his finger and sandals on his feet.
Take the fattened calf and slaughter it. Then let us celebrate with a feast, because this son of mine was dead, and
has come to life again; he was lost, and has been found.'
Then the celebration began."

"Now the older son had been out in the field and, on
his way back, as he neared the house, he heard the sound
of music and dancing. He called one of the servants and
asked what this might mean. The servant said to him,
'Your brother has returned and your father has slaughtered
the fattened calf because he has him back safe and sound.'
He became angry, and when he refused to enter the house,
his father came out and pleaded with him. He said to his
father in reply, 'Look, all these years I served you and not
once did I disobey your orders; yet you never gave me even
a young goat to feast on with my friends. But when your
son returns who swallowed up your property with pros-
titutes, for him you slaughter the fattened calf.' He said
to him, 'My son, you are here with me always; everything
I have is yours. But now we must celebrate and rejoice,

because your brother was dead and has come to life again; he was lost and has been found.'"

There are many stories in the Gospels where Jesus forgives people, sometimes in connection with a cure, sometimes provoking outrage among Pharisees and other critics. The parable of the prodigal son, unique to Luke, is the most extravagant example of forgiveness. A young man, too impatient to await his father's death, first arrogantly demands, then squanders, his expected inheritance, after which he is mercifully and even joyfully welcomed home by his father.

The three characters in this story invite us to reflect on forgiveness in different ways: the son who repents of his sin after experiencing its consequences; the embittered brother who insists on justice, not mercy; and the father who forgives them both out of a magnitude of love that is almost beyond imagination: God's forgiveness, God's love.

On the cross, Jesus forgave those who killed him (Luke 23:34). Before that, he told his disciples to forgive "not seven times but seventy-seven times" (Matthew 18:21–22), and he taught us to pray, every day, "Forgive us our trespasses as we forgive those who trespass against us"—just as the heartbroken father in the parable forgave his prodigal son.

Forgiving is often hardest when we have been hurt by someone close to us. The result can be years of alienation.

Parents and children are embittered. Siblings don't speak to each other for many years, even after they've forgotten what the original quarrel was about. Friendships are ended by misunderstanding. Professional relationships are ruined by competition. No one wants to make the first move toward reconciliation.

How do we start? Not just by saying, "I'm going to forgive," although that's an important first step. When we are hurt or angry, true forgiveness requires a change of heart. If there is someone you need to forgive, whether for something small or something important, ask God for the grace to forgive, as God has forgiven you.

The other side of this coin, of course, is seeking forgiveness: being forgiven. This means not only asking God's forgiveness (the subject of the next chapter) but also humbling ourselves to ask forgiveness from someone we have hurt. When we've done wrong, we ought to make amends. If someone steals money, it ought to be repaid. If we steal someone's peace or happiness, even briefly, shouldn't we make restitution? Just telling God we're sorry doesn't make the injured person whole.

PRAYER STARTERS

1. Which of the three characters in this parable do you identify with, and why?

2. Which is more important to you: justice or mercy? Why do you think this is so?

3. Can you reconcile justice with the father's extravagant mercy? Why, or why not?

4. Is there someone, living or dead, whom you need to forgive? Who is it, and what wrong do you need to forgive?

5. Is there someone, living or dead, whose forgiveness you need to ask? Who is it, and for what do you need forgiveness?

6. Pray with Luke 6:36: "Be merciful, just as [also] your Father is merciful."

17

The Call to Repentance:
King David * Peter

Scripture: 2 Samuel 11:2–4; 12:1–7, 13

One evening David rose from his bed and strolled about on the roof of the king's house. From the roof he saw a woman bathing; she was very beautiful. David sent people to inquire about the woman and was told, "She is Bathsheba, daughter of Eliam, and wife of Uriah the Hittite, Joab's armor-bearer." Then David sent messengers and took her.

———

[When Bathsheba became pregnant, David first schemed to conceal his sin (2 Samuel 11:6–13); then had Uriah killed (11:14–21) and married Bathsheba (11:27).]

———

The LORD sent Nathan to David, and when he came to him, he said: "Tell me how you judge this case: In a certain town there were two men, one rich, the other poor. The rich man had flocks and herds in great numbers. But the poor man had nothing at all except one little ewe lamb that he had bought. He nourished her, and she grew up with him and his children. Of what little he had she ate; from his own cup she drank; in his bosom she slept; she was like a daughter to him. Now, a visitor came to the rich man, but he spared his own flocks and herds to prepare a meal for the traveler who had come to him: he took the poor man's ewe lamb and prepared it for the one who had come to him." David grew very angry with that man and said to Nathan: "As the LORD lives, the man who has done this deserves death! He shall make fourfold restitution for the lamb because he has done this and was unsparing." Then Nathan said to David: "You are the man!"

———

Then David said to Nathan, "I have sinned against the LORD." Nathan answered David: "For his part, the LORD has removed your sin. You shall not die."

Over the centuries, artists and scholars have often interpreted Bathsheba as a temptress or seductress or even as one conspiring for power. With our twenty-first-century understanding of power relationships, we are better able to understand that sex between a powerful king and a female subject was exploitation and abuse. It's difficult, then, to identify with David: none of us is likely to feel any empathy with a man guilty of rape, murder, and abuse of authority. But that is not the point of the story. It is, of course, the last verse that draws us and consoles us: once David admitted his sin, terrible as it was, God's forgiveness was immediate.

Most of the world's major religions have some form of rite for the remission of sin, such as the sacrament of reconciliation for Roman Catholics, the repentance prescribed during the ten days between Rosh Hashanah and Yom Kippur for Jews, and the ritual of bathing in the Ganges River for Hindus. All these rituals require some form of self-examination: It isn't easy to admit, even to ourselves, that we have done wrong. The promise of God's mercy—shown immediately to David despite his great sins—should give us the courage to face our consciences.

PRAYER STARTERS

1. David, who had gone to great lengths to conceal his sin (see 2 Samuel 11:6–25), needed the help of the prophet Nathan to open his eyes to his culpability. What transgressions in your past have you had difficulty facing? Pray for the grace to know your sins and trust in God's mercy.

2. David's sin did not go unpunished. (The full details of his treachery and punishment take up all of chapters 11 and 12 of the second book of Samuel.) Today, unlike ancient peoples, we don't expect God to strike us dead if we sin. How seriously do we take the need for atonement?

3. Pray Psalm 51:3–6, 11–15, a penitential psalm, attributed to David "when Nathan the prophet came to him after he had gone in to Bathsheba":

> Have mercy on me, God, in accord with your
>   merciful love;
> in your abundant compassion blot out my
>   transgressions.
> Thoroughly wash away my guilt;
> and from my sin cleanse me.
> For I know my transgressions;
> my sin is always before me.
> Against you, you alone have I sinned;
> I have done what is evil in your eyes
> So that you are just in your word,
> and without reproach in your judgment.

Behold, I was born in guilt,
in sin my mother conceived me. . . .
Turn away your face from my sins;
blot out all my iniquities.
A clean heart create for me, God;
renew within me a steadfast spirit.
Do not drive me from before your face,
nor take from me your holy spirit.
Restore to me the gladness of your salvation;
uphold me with a willing spirit.
I will teach the wicked your ways,
that sinners may return to you.

4. Pray one of the other penitential psalms of David: 6, 32, 38, 102, or 143.

Peter

Scripture: Luke 22:54–62

After arresting him they led him away and took him into the house of the high priest; Peter was following at a distance. They lit a fire in the middle of the courtyard and sat around it, and Peter sat down with them. When a maid saw him seated in the light, she looked intently at him and said, "This man too was with him." But he denied it saying, "Woman, I do not know him." A short while later someone else saw him and said, "You too are one of them"; but Peter answered, "My friend, I am not." About an hour later, still another insisted, "Assuredly, this man too was with him, for he also is a Galilean." But Peter said, "My friend, I do not know what you are talking about." Just as he was saying this, the cock crowed, and the Lord turned and looked at Peter; and Peter remembered the word of the Lord, how he had said to him, "Before the cock crows today, you will deny me three times." He went out and began to weep bitterly.

All four evangelists tell the story of Peter's denial (Matthew 26:57–58, 69–75; Mark 14:53–54, 67–72; John 18:15–18, 25–27), but only Luke includes the telling detail that "the Lord turned and looked at Peter."

PRAYER STARTERS

1. Imagine Jesus looking at you. Can you ask mercy for your sins? If not, why not?

2. Revisit the story of the prodigal son, Luke 15:11–32, in the previous chapter. How can you experience God's mercy as he did?

3. Pray Psalm 130, a plea for God's mercy attributed to David. Substitute yourself for the references to Israel:

> Out of the depths I call to you, LORD;
> Lord, hear my cry!
> May your ears be attentive
> to my cry for mercy.
> If you, LORD, keep account of sins,
> Lord, who can stand?
> But with you is forgiveness
> and so you are revered.
> I wait for the LORD,
> my soul waits
> and I hope for his word.
> My soul looks for the Lord
> more than sentinels for daybreak.
> More than sentinels for daybreak,
> let Israel hope in the LORD,
> For with the LORD is mercy,
> with him is plenteous redemption,
> And he will redeem Israel
> from all its sins.

18

The Call to Witness:
Joseph of Arimathea

Scripture: John 19:38–42

After this, Joseph of Arimathea, secretly a disciple of Jesus for fear of the Jews, asked Pilate if he could remove the body of Jesus. And Pilate permitted it. So he came and took his body. Nicodemus, the one who had first come to him at night, also came bringing a mixture of myrrh and aloes weighing about one hundred pounds. They took the body of Jesus and bound it with burial cloths along with the spices, according to the Jewish burial custom. Now in the place where he had been crucified there was a garden, and in the garden a new tomb, in which no one had yet been buried. So they laid Jesus there because of the Jewish preparation day; for the tomb was close by.

Joseph of Arimathea is a bit player in the drama of Jesus' life but one important enough to be mentioned in all four Gospels as the man who claimed the body of Jesus and buried it in a new tomb. Matthew says he was "a rich man" (27:57);

Mark describes him as "a distinguished member of the council" (15:43); and Luke adds that he was "a virtuous and righteous man" who, "though he was a member of the council, had not consented to their plan of action" (23:50–51). Although we do not know his age, his position of leadership is strong evidence that he was of mature years.

John is the only evangelist who identifies him as a secret disciple, "for fear of the Jews." His fear was certainly not unfounded. Even before Jesus' entry into Jerusalem, the likelihood of his arrest was evidently well known, because people were speculating about whether he would come up for the Passover (John 11:55–57). Jesus mostly stayed out of sight until his arrest. Peter denied knowing him, and all the male disciples except John fled in fear. They were still living in fear when the risen Jesus appeared to them, and they seem to have remained in hiding until they received the Holy Spirit (see Acts 2:1–4). Joseph of Arimathea evidently shared these fears; he had not come out openly as a disciple before the execution of Jesus. As a rich and distinguished man, he had a lot to lose, and now that Jesus was dead, he had nothing to gain. Yet in a moment of great courage, he went to Pilate in order to give Jesus proper burial.

He went even further, with the help of Nicodemus, wrapping the body with linen and spices. This was normally women's work. We have no clue as to why Joseph undertook it. Perhaps he underestimated the courage of Jesus' women disciples and worried that Jesus would be subject to the final indignity of neglect. Perhaps it was a further expression of the powerful emotion that led him to undertake the burial in the first place.

Whatever the reason, his action was even more visible than the request he made of Pilate. Overcoming his fears, as well as his sadness and feelings of loss, he bore public witness to his faith in Jesus.

Where did this courage come from? God gives grace to whom he wishes, when he wishes; it isn't earned, and it can't be explained. What is clear is that Joseph experienced grace at just the time and place that it was needed. A lifetime of "awaiting the kingdom of God" had not previously led him to follow Jesus openly; yet now, when all appeared lost, he found the courage for public witness.

He may well have paid a price for his courage. There is an ancient legend, probably derived from the apocryphal "Gospel of Nicodemus," that the Jewish authorities were furious with Joseph, and imprisoned him for a time. Whether the legend has any basis in fact, it is clear in our own times that bearing witness to the truth often has serious consequences, including prison, suppression, or even martyrdom.

Rosa Parks (1913–2005) knew she would likely be arrested for refusing to give up her seat on the bus to a white passenger. She nevertheless decided it was time to witness to the evil of the Jim Crow laws, as did many civil rights activists who followed her example in the 1960s. Irena Sendler (1910–2008), a Polish Catholic social worker who rescued 2,500 Jewish children from the Warsaw Ghetto, was imprisoned and tortured, and her story was suppressed by the communist government of Poland. Sendler's story was largely unknown in the United States until the research of three high school girls in Kansas shed light on her life. Blessed Franz Jägerstätter (1907–1943) knew that the penalty for refusing to serve in the Nazi army was death, but he refused to participate in evil. Today he is a candidate for sainthood, and people are debating and developing new ways to witness to peace in a world where it is increasingly endangered.

Most of us don't face martyrdom, imprisonment, or other such dramatic choices as a result of living our faith. We may well shudder at the thought; it may be easier to identify with the fearful disciples in the Upper Room.

But we are all called to witness to our faith, by what we say, by what we do, and above all by the way we live. In a secular society where religion seems increasingly countercultural, this may be as simple as practicing our faith openly.

That doesn't mean flaunting it or proselytizing or saying "Merry Christmas" to people who are Jewish or Muslim. It does mean being alert to the voice of the Holy Spirit, and then living what we believe.

PRAYER STARTERS

1. Have you ever been challenged by someone who does not share your beliefs? If so, how have you responded? Is there a better response?

2. What cultural influences prevent you from living your faith as fully and actively as possible?

3. What moral or social issues are most important to you? How can you get involved: can you write, speak, join a support group, or participate in some form of action?

19

The Call to Courage:
The Woman with a Flow of Blood

Scripture: Mark 5:25–34

There was a woman afflicted with hemorrhages for twelve years. She had suffered greatly at the hands of many doctors and had spent all that she had. Yet she was not helped but only grew worse. She had heard about Jesus and came up behind him in the crowd and touched his cloak. She said, "If I but touch his clothes, I shall be cured." Immediately her flow of blood dried up. She felt in her body that she was healed of her affliction. Jesus, aware at once that power had gone out from him, turned around in the crowd and asked, "Who has touched my clothes?" But his disciples said to him, "You see how the crowd is pressing upon you, and yet you ask, 'Who touched me?'" And he looked around to see who had done it. The woman, realizing what had happened to her, approached in fear and trembling. She fell down before Jesus and told him the whole truth. He said to her, "Daughter, your faith has saved you. Go in peace and be cured of your affliction."

Plainly, the woman in this episode suffered greatly from her illness. More serious than her physical ailment was her virtual ostracism from the community because of it. A "flow of blood" was a grave problem under the Mosaic Law. The rules for ritual purity were complex and extremely detailed. The woman who experienced a flow of blood was not only "unclean" but so was any bed on which she lay, any chair on which she sat, and any person who touched any of those objects (Leviticus 15:25–27).

The effect of these rules is mind-boggling. In her own home, no one could touch her or her bed or chair. If she was married, she could not sleep in the same bed with her husband, lest he be rendered unclean. Everyone in the household ran the constant risk of ritual impurity. For seven days, that might have been bearable, but for twelve years? Could she have been any more unwelcome if she were a leper? The pre-scientific medicine of the day only added to her sufferings, as did the cost of fruitless treatments. It took great courage to endure so much pain for so many years.

Then she "heard about Jesus," and believed—hoped against hope—that he could cure her. She found the courage to touch his cloak, even knowing that as she did so she would render him unclean. Thus, when he asked who had touched him, she "approached in fear and trembling." It took great courage both to act on her faith in his healing power and to overcome the humiliation of discussing it in public. But her greatest courage was in the patience and perseverance with which she had suffered illness and ostracism for twelve years.

In our own times, institutionalized ostracism of the sick occurs from time to time, as in the brutal treatment of some victims of AIDS in the 1980s. Much more common is the experience of people whose isolation is a kind of collateral damage of their illness. A woman undergoing chemotherapy who loses all her hair may no longer be comfortable going out in public. Someone with any kind of debilitating illness may not have the energy to socialize. Even people with loving families find that, in many ways, life goes on without them.

It's easy to think of courage as involving some kind of heroic action or as speaking truth to power. For the sick, courage may be very private, silent, and unobserved by anyone but God. All suffering is a call to courage.

PRAYER STARTERS

1. Imagine touching the hem of Jesus' cloak. What does it feel like? He turns and looks at you. What do you say to him?

2. Most of us understand intellectually that suffering is part of the human condition, but we have more difficulty when it touches us. Talk to God about your own suffering or that of someone close to you. Ask to see the grace in it.

20

The Call to Let Go: Peter

Scripture: John 21:18–19

"Amen, amen, I say to you, when you were younger, you used to dress yourself and go where you wanted; but when you grow old, you will stretch out your hands, and someone else will dress you and lead you where you do not want to go." He said this signifying by what kind of death he would glorify God. And when he had said this, he said to him, "Follow me."

This scene takes place on the shore of the Sea of Galilee, when the risen Jesus appears to seven disciples. Three times he asks Peter if he loves him; three times Peter protests that he does; three times Jesus instructs him to feed his lambs and sheep (John 21:15–17). Then Jesus suddenly changes the subject: it isn't going to be easy. The evangelist interprets Jesus' words as predicting Peter's martyrdom; the tradition is that he was crucified head-down in Rome. To the modern reader, the first sentence is more likely to suggest the loss of independence that comes "when you grow old."

As we age, most of us become more dependent on others, and that is definitely "where [we] do not want to go." For many people, this is a source of unspoken fear. It's common to hear someone say, "I don't want to be a burden"; often what they really mean is "I'm terrified of losing my independence."

How do we deal with the diminishment that comes with age: impaired mobility, the need to give up driving, or the loss of friends and people we love? It's a sad reality that the longer we live, the more people we outlive. Yet in these very circumstances Jesus said to Peter, "Follow me." He extends the same invitation to us.

It's hard to hear a call to discipleship in painful losses and unspoken fears. Many people who are sick or grieving experience a call to share in the sufferings of Jesus. In Mark's Gospel, Jesus tells the crowd: "Whoever wishes to come after me must deny himself, take up his cross, and follow me" (8:34). Luke adds a little more emphasis: "If anyone wishes to come after me, he must deny himself and take up his cross *daily* and follow me" (9:23, emphasis added). If we live a life of discipleship, following Jesus, sooner or later we have to follow him to the Cross.

How do we pray about that?

One way is to be with Jesus in the Garden of Gethsemane. Jesus knew fear—fear of what he had to endure on the way to death. In Luke's version (22:39–46), an angel came to strengthen him. Note that the angel didn't take away the pain but strengthened Jesus to bear it. For us, whatever form our sufferings may take, this scene can remind us to look for the grace in all things.

Another approach is embodied in a prayer of St. Ignatius of Loyola called Suscipe, which means "take." Here is a modern translation:

> Take, Lord, and receive all my liberty, my memory, my understanding, and my entire will—all that I have and call my own. You have given it all to me. To you, Lord, I return it. Everything is yours; do with it what you will. Give me only your love and your grace. That is enough for me. [Spiritual Exercises § 234, Fleming translation]

One way to understand this prayer, at any age, is as a reminder of our total dependence on God. We're not asking for a particular form of suffering. In general, that's a bad idea. We have enough to deal with in accepting the pain and the trials God chooses to send us. What we're asking for is the grace to recognize our total dependence on God, to recognize that our memory, our understanding, our will—everything that makes us human—is God's gift.

PRAYER STARTERS

1. Pray for the grace to be willing to share the Passion of Christ. Choose one episode from any of the Passion narratives: Matthew 26:31–27:56; Mark 14:27–15:39; Luke 22:31–23:49; John 18:1–19:37. Focus on images (imaginative prayer) or words (*lectio divina*), as explained in chapter 1. Choose a fairly narrow episode, such as Jesus before Herod, the carrying of the cross, or Pilate's exchanges with the Jewish mob—whatever seems to resonate with you—but don't try to focus on more than one episode at a time. The rest of the chapter will still be there next time.

2. Pray with John 14:1–4 or Luke 22:39–46. Ask for the grace to trust in God's mercy in times of suffering.

3. Try to imagine your total dependence on God. Think about how helpless you were as a baby. Your parents cared for you when you could do nothing for yourself except to cry when you needed something. As adults who raise families, run businesses, and take care of other people, we are every bit as dependent on God—except that he knows our needs before we ever open our mouths.

   If you have a cat or dog, a perfect, beautiful creature who embodies God's love, think of the animal's dependence on you as a metaphor for your relationship to God. You give it food, shelter, medical care, and love. Even though you always try to do what's best for it, your gifts aren't always appreciated. My own two cats used to engage in antiphonal meowing when I put them in the car to take them to the vet. Think for a moment of how much we love our pets, even when they aren't acting lovable, and imagine how to multiply it to think of God's love for us.

4. Listen to each beat of your heart and thank God for it. Pay attention to your breathing and thank God for each breath.

5. What is your greatest fear? Name it and ask the God who loves you for the grace to let go.

6. Pray Psalm 71, in which the psalmist reviews how God has sustained him from youth to old age. What do you want "all generations to come" to know about God's goodness?

21

The Call to Eternal Life: Simeon

Scripture: Luke 2:22–32

When the days were completed for their purification according to the law of Moses, they took him up to Jerusalem to present him to the Lord, just as it is written in the law of the Lord, "Every male that opens the womb shall be consecrated to the Lord," and to offer the sacrifice of "a pair of turtle doves or two young pigeons," in accordance with the dictate in the law of the Lord.

Now there was a man in Jerusalem whose name was Simeon. This man was righteous and devout, awaiting the consolation of Israel, and the holy Spirit was upon him. It had been revealed to him by the holy Spirit that he should not see death before he had seen the Messiah of the Lord. He came in the Spirit into the temple; and when the parents brought in the child Jesus to perform the custom of the law in regard to him, he took him into his arms and blessed God, saying:

"Now, Master, you may let your servant go in peace, according to your word, for my eyes have seen your salvation, which you prepared in sight of all the peoples, a light for revelation to the Gentiles, and glory for your people Israel."

Simeon's prayer, often called by its Latin name, Nunc Dimittis, is included in Night Prayer in the Roman Catholic Liturgy of the Hours and in Evensong in the churches of the Anglican Communion. Significantly, it is prayed at the end of the day, an obvious metaphor for the end of earthly life. Simeon's peaceful readiness for eternal life has been meaningful for generations of Christians.

Luke does not tell us Simeon's age, but "it had been revealed to him by the holy Spirit that he should not see death before he had seen the Messiah of the Lord." In other words, he was old enough to be thinking about how much time he had left on earth and to be worrying about whether he would die too soon and miss what he had been waiting and praying for all his life. Opinions about what happens to the soul after death were divided among devout Jews of the time: the Pharisees believed in eternal life, while the Sadducees vigorously rejected it. Whatever Simeon's views on the issue, he was "awaiting the consolation of Israel."

Led to the Temple by the Holy Spirit and, like Anna, given the grace immediately to recognize the infant Jesus, he burst out in a prophetic song of praise and thanksgiving. Like many of the prophets who preceded him, he may not have known the full meaning of words such as "salvation" and "a light for revelation to the Gentiles," but it was enough for him to know that God's promise had been fulfilled.

That knowledge filled him with peace. After a "righteous and devout" lifetime of waiting and hoping, he was ready to accept death. He was called to look forward to eternal life, and he did so with gratitude and hope.

Whatever else we're called to do, as Christians and disciples, we're called to look at the end of the road and face it without fear. That isn't easy. We live in a society that in many ways is in denial about death. The messages we get would have been familiar to the Sadducees of Jesus' time: Don't think about it. Death is the end. Live for now. As Christians, though, we know that death is a part of life and that life continues after death.

We're not sure what form that life may take, but we are sure that Jesus promised us eternal life. He made that promise explicitly and unambiguously, over and over. John's Gospel gives the promise particular prominence: in Jesus' conversation with the Samaritan woman at the well (John 4:14); in the "bread of life" discourse (John 6:48–51); just before raising Lazarus from the dead (John 11:24–26); and in one of the most familiar passages in the entire New Testament, "For God so loved the world that he gave his only Son, so that everyone who believes in him might not perish but might have eternal life" (John 3:16).

One of the most interesting examples is found in Luke 20:27–38. One of the Sadducees put to Jesus a hypothetical question about a woman who married seven brothers in succession, in accordance with the custom that called for a dead man's surviving brother to marry his widow: "Now at the resurrection whose wife will that woman be?"

One can almost hear the conscious effort at patience in Jesus' reply:

> "They can no longer die, for they are like angels; and they are the children of God because they are the ones who will rise. That the dead will rise even Moses made known in the passage about the bush, when he called 'Lord' the God of Abraham, the God of Isaac, and the God of Jacob. and he is not God of the dead, but of the living, for to him all are alive."

So we will rise "like angels" and as "children of God"—whatever that may mean. We too are called to believe in the promise of eternal life and to look forward to it in peace.

PRAYER STARTERS

1. Pray Simeon's prayer at the end of your day.

2. Pray with one of the Scripture passages dealing with eternal life, such as the ones mentioned above, or Matthew 19:27–29; John 14:1–6; Revelation 21:1–4, 22–25.

3. Simeon was at peace with the idea of death. Are you? If not, why not? Talk to God about it.

4. Pray the prayer attributed to St. Teresa of Ávila:

   Let nothing disturb you; let nothing affright you
   All passes away
   God only shall stay
   Patience wins all
   Who has God lacks nothing, for God is his all.

Epilogue: Prayer of an Aging Disciple

Lord, grant me the grace
    to live in the present and recognize what is possible
    to look to the future and trust you
    to be silent, and hear your voice in the stillness
    to do what you ask without arguing
    to humbly adapt to radical change
    to serve, and to graciously accept being served
    to give generously
    to be ever grateful for all your generous gifts
    to use all my gifts in whatever form of service you ask of me
    to rejoice in all the graces you have given me
    to forgive and ask forgiveness
    to be sorry for all the times I have not responded to your call
    to live in a way that bears witness to you
    to have courage in times of trial
    to let go of all that keeps me from drawing ever closer to you
    to look forward to the future with hope
    and to be ever surprised as you make all things new.
Amen.

Further Reading

Praying with Scripture

Lewis, Albert Micah. *The Lord Is My Shepherd: Psalms to Accompany Us on Our Journey Through Aging.* Grand Rapids, MI: Eerdmans, 2003.

Martin, James. *Jesus: A Pilgrimage.* New York: HarperCollins, 2014.

Merton, Thomas. *Praying the Psalms.* Collegeville, MN: Liturgical Press, 1956.

Mestre, Gabriel. *Pray with the Bible, Meditate with the Word: The Exciting World of Lectio Divina.* New York: American Bible Society, 2010.

Ignatian Spirituality

Fleming, David L. *Draw Me into Your Friendship: The Spiritual Exercises, a Literal Translation and a Contemporary Reading.* St. Louis, MO: Institute of Jesuit Sources, 1996.

Fleming, David L. *What Is Ignatian Spirituality?* Chicago: Loyola Press, 2008.

Manney, Jim. *A Simple Life-Changing Prayer: Discovering the Power of St. Ignatius Loyola's Examen.* Chicago: Loyola Press, 2011.

Silf, Margaret. *Inner Compass: An Invitation to Ignatian Spirituality.* Chicago: Loyola Press, 2007.

https://www.ignatianspirituality.com/

Spirituality of Aging

Chittister, Joan. *The Gift of Years: Growing Older Gracefully.* Katonah, NY: Bluebridge Books, 2008.

Pope Francis and Friends. *Sharing the Wisdom of Time.* Chicago: Loyola Press, 2018. https://www.sharingwisdomoftime.com/sharing/ (Upload your own story.)

Twentieth-Century Role Models

Blessed Titus Brandsma: Dolle, Constant. *Encountering God in the Abyss: Titus Brandsma's Spiritual Journey.* Vriend, John, translator. Leuven, Belgium: Peeters, 2002.

Blessed Franz Jägerstätter: Zahn, Gordon. *In Solitary Witness: The Life and Death of Franz Jägerstätter.* Springfield, IL: Templegate, 1986.

Rosa Parks: Brinkley, Douglas. *Rosa Parks: A Life.* New York: Penguin Books, 2005.

Irena Sendler: Mayer, Jack. *Life in a Jar: The Irena Sendler Project.* Middlebury, VT: Long Trail Press, 2011.

Caregiving

Craghan, John F. *I Was Ill and You Cared for Me: Biblical Reflections on Serving the Physically and Mentally Impaired.* Collegeville, MN: Liturgical Press, 2014.

Driscoll, Marilyn. *Devotions for Caregivers: A Month's Supply of Prayer.* Mahwah, NJ: Paulist Press, 2006.

About the Author

Barbara Lee is a practicing spiritual director who lives in New York City. She is a retired attorney, a former U.S. magistrate judge, and a long-serving member of the Ignatian Volunteer Corps—an organization of retired people inspired by Ignatian spirituality who perform volunteer work among the poor. She is the author of *God Isn't Finished with Me Yet*.